Copyright © 2018 by Larry Zielke
Story Editor R. Fernandez
All Rights Reserved
Art by Herald Entertainment, Inc.
Printed in China
First Printing: June 2018
ISBN: 978-1-947774-80-3

Don't Ever Park Your Camel
on a Busy, Crowded Street!

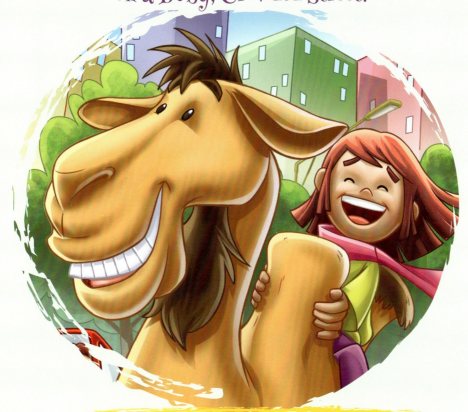

A Tale of True Friendship

Written by Larry Zielke

My camel's name is Claude
He's clumsy but he's sweet;
He's also the nicest camel
That you'd ever hope to meet.

He smiles real big when greeting you
He'll stop and shake your hand;
Sometimes he acts real foolish
Showering you with sand.

We were minding our own business—
I was shopping for some toys,
When I turned away I didn't see
An approaching group of boys.

Now it's true that Claude is clumsy;
He may stumble but not fall.
But he understands most everything.
He's as smart as he is tall.

Soon a crowd had gathered
To watch the silly sight.
"This camel thinks he's better than me!"
He said, "And that's not right!"

Then a brave voice in the crowd cried out,
"Let the camel speak his part!
For though I've never met one,
Now's a good time to start!"

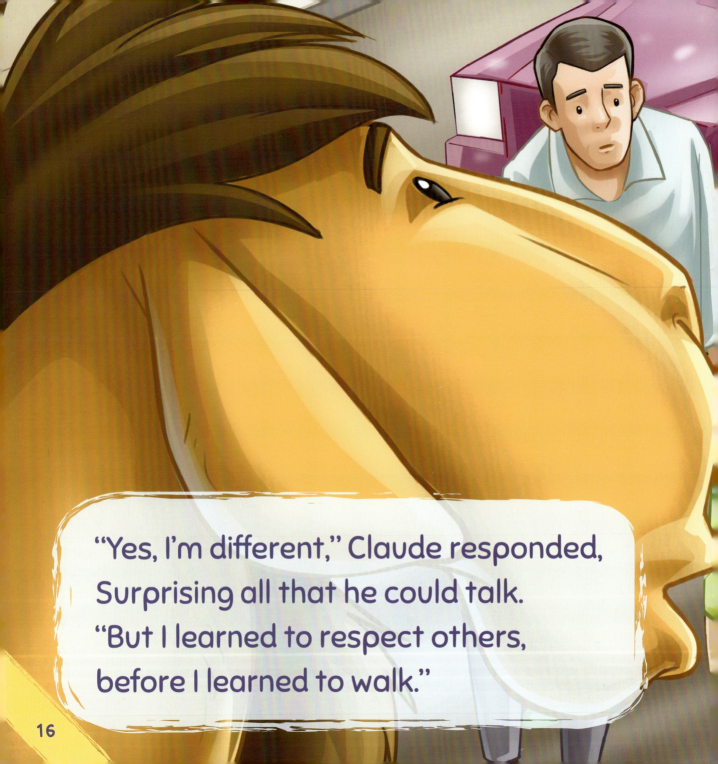

"Yes, I'm different," Claude responded,
Surprising all that he could talk.
"But I learned to respect others,
before I learned to walk."

The gathered crowd let out a cheer.
The bully slipped away.
Though Claude didn't feel like a hero,
The crowd treated him that way.

"Growing up, my parents taught me,
We camels have a code:
Never hurt or make fun of others,
Especially those that you don't know."

So I had to learn the hard way
With cars honking, *beep, beep, beep!*
Don't ever park your camel
On a busy, crowded street!

Something to Talk About

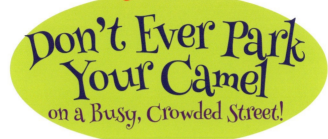

- What do you like about this story and why?

- Why do you think the bully was making fun of the camel?

- Why did the bully run away when the crowd cheered for Claude?

- Discuss with your parent or teacher what you should do if someone says something mean to you or to one of your friends?

Make-believe stories are a fun way to entertain children while teaching them to make right choices in real life situations.

"The ZooMaster from Mars"
▼
Helps children be content with who they are, and not to compare themselves negatively with others.

"Don't Ever Park Your Camel on a Busy, Crowded Street"
▼
Teaches children to respect others— even those they may not know.

For more information please visit:
www.LZBooks.com